Nana Says!

Everything I Know

I Learned On

The Farm

———————

linda nickey

Copyright © 2012 Linda Nickey

Published by Linda Nickey
Author, *Make A Plan (MAP),* published 2005

lmnickey@aol.com
www.lindanickey.com
925-586-5236

Editing by Andrea Susan Glass, www.WritersWay.com
Cover design by Claudia Chalberg, www.Visionew.com
Cover photo by Paul Bevins

All rights reserved. No part of this publication may be reproduced, stored in a retrieval system, or transmitted by any means, electronic, mechanical, photocopying, recording, or otherwise, without written permission from the author and publisher.

ISBN# 978-0-9786749-0-8

*This book is dedicated to my beautiful daughter,
Jennifer and wonderful grandsons,
Jacob and Samuel.*

Contents

Introduction 5

One: Childhood Stories—The Building Blocks .. 11

Two: The Tween Years—A Confusing And Chaotic Time 72

Three: Memories Of The Farm Fun Times 80

Four: The Teen Years Brought Many Changes ... 96

Five: Lessons From My Heart And What I Have Learned That Is Important 103

Six: My Life In Balance—The Steps 112

Seven: Testimonials—My Friends Sharing Their Thoughts 118

About The Author... 132

Introduction

I've written this book hoping it will help a few people along the way. Maybe it will show the value of determination, courage, desire, hope, perseverance, and much more. I have a strong desire to write about my childhood stories, the stories that no one can recount as I will. This book has been written first and foremost for my daughter and my grandsons. I'm hopeful others will enjoy it was well.

Author, international trainer, and motivational speaker Les Brown says, "If you don't tell your story, you leave no legacy. People want to hear your story."

So I have been writing!

Each story has a lesson contained in it. Of course starting at the young age of five and so on I didn't really know the lessons I was learning, yet I somehow felt I was learning important "stuff" and not all of it did I like at the time. The many lessons learned on the farm have brought me to where I am today.

It was early in my life when I understood the value of listening intently and observing behaviors. These were skills that I didn't realize then would prepare me for later years to deal with difficult situations. I was very aware and tuned in way beyond my young years. My home was a pretty volatile environment, and I understood even then how I could be of value during some of the upheaval going on around me. I found by paying close attention to words, actions, and looks, I could sometimes help deter certain unhealthy situation just by "distracting" what was going on.

It's not easy to turn a negative frightening situation into a positive learning one, yet it can be done.

Growing up too fast too young is not healthy as it takes away childhood innocence, trust, and a feeling of security. Gaining self confidence, feeling safe, speaking honestly, and having the ability to allow raw emotion to come out are all part of what a healthy family environment can do for children. When some, if not all, of that is stripped away, it may leave the child vulnerable and they begin "story telling games." As children, we make things up that seem like what they may be, because we don't have the maturity to know for sure what the "real" story is. Often we pretend, becoming the person it seems we need to be to "fit" into the situation.

Some of you reading this book may have situations in your life where you feel or have felt unsafe, unable to be authentic, unsure of what was/is real, and have a lack of trust in people. The question you may ask yourself is, "Is this the right place, time, and circumstances for me to be authentic, to be the real me?" Perhaps you put your mind into full gear to look, listen, and pay close attention to signs and gather clues as to how you should be. You may search through your "head library" for similar situations and ask what worked best then. In truth, that may be the worst way to manage the situation as it could start a process of not being authentic, which can then lead to other problems—all the very things you're trying to move away from.

Good news! As we get older and wiser, we learn and realize we can change the things we no longer want in our life, the things perhaps holding us back or making us feel less than. Of course, it takes work as most things do that are truly important to us. It's worth the effort it takes to get such a feeling of accomplishment. When you say, "I'm changing my direction; this no longer serves me," your life can and will change. And you may say, "I'm getting back on track, the track I want to be on, the track I had hoped and planned for." Watch out as the flood gates open to bring to you that which you need. Once you get to this point, you're on full steam ahead, and whatever you've dealt with in the past is just that, the past. Your past brought you to this point in time, and you're well prepared. This is your NOW time, and it's your time to create the life and dreams you desire!

Following each story I have a few thoughts on what I feel as an adult may have been my life lesson(s) learned to prepare me for later years. The journal note space that follows is to provide you with an opportunity to write down thoughts that come to mind for you on any situation you may be dealing with now.

I have an inspirational quote before most stories by one of my favorite mentors, Les Brown. He's helped me through life with many quotes, and this one in particular, "It's Possible", I use often when things seem very hard and I see no answers yet.

Les Brown says:
How you live your life is as a result of the story you believe about yourself. Do your thoughts, actions, inner and outer conversations, and associations speak to the value that you place on your own life story?

Write an unforgettable powerful epic life story with your own pen...worthy of a Pulitzer prize...an Oscar...or perhaps a Nobel Prize. Choose to see your life as an amazing discovery and adventure into the extraordinary versions of you! You must live your legacy...in order to leave a legacy! Live full out!!

Another of my favorite mentors and inspirational leaders is Glenna Salsbury, the author of *The Art of the Fresh Start*. She's an international keynote speaker, workshop leader, and spiritual coach. I've known Glenna for over 30 years, and I know she lives by her four principles.

Glenna inspired me to write this book. I live my life using her four principles as my life guide. Glenna's mission is "*Make people glad they saw you*", and her four essential principles are:

1) Be interested in others. Ask questions and listen to the answers.
2) Be willing to display enthusiastic support for others.
3) Find ways to rekindle individual enthusiasm for life and work.
4) Help people expand their horizons for what *might be* instead of what *is*.

> *"My life journey has no roadmap;*
> *no one has traveled in my steps."*
> ~ linda nickey

"*Everything I know I learned on the farm.*"

I'm very excited to have you join me for a few childhood stories about my life growing up on the farm! The stories are the way I remember them and at the age I believe I was at the time. Now that I'm a NANA, I thought I would share these stories with you—whatever age you are as the lessons are universal. I've done my best to keep the stories in sequence for easier reading. I hope you enjoy the journey.

> *"Goals help you channel your energy into action."*
> ~ Les Brown

ONE:

Childhood Stories—The Building Blocks

> *"Don't let someone else's opinion of you become your reality."*
> ~ Les Brown

Kindergarten in Rural South Dakota

I was so excited to go to school with my "big" sister. I thought it was fun to be able to do what she was doing. I wasn't ready for the rude, unkind teacher...

I was five, and the last two weeks of school in the one room schoolhouse I went to was kindergarten time. So I went with my sister who was one year older. I was getting into the whole thing, trying to do what everyone else was doing so I would fit in. The teacher asked a question, and many hands went up, so I put mine up too. Soon the teacher asked, "And Linda, what do you think the answer is?" I said, "I don't know. Everyone put their hands up, so I did too." She scolded me in front of all 17 classmates ages five to 14, grades one to eight. I didn't cry, yet I knew I'd done something very wrong; she made that clear

Really, oh my, what we remember. A good thing to keep in mind is that at all ages, words are powerful.

Life Lessons

Be brave even if someone makes you feel bad
You'll never know the answer to everything,
and it's okay to be wrong
New situations are exciting; we may make
mistakes and that's okay

_____
_____
_____
_____
_____
_____
_____
_____

> *"Forgive yourself for your faults and your mistakes and move on."*
> ~ Les Brown

Did I Swallow the Safety Pin?

I was scared I was doing something I wasn't suppose to be doing and had to tell.

Many times I had watched my Mom put safety pins in between her teeth when changing my younger brother's diapers. So when it was time to play "dolls" with my sister, we of course had the babies wet their pants so we could change the little makeshift hankie diapers we had made. Now we had been told of all the dangers of putting pins in our mouth, the most of which was if you swallow one it could end up in your lung and may even cause death. It sounded pretty scary to me.

One day, I did the unthinkable. I put the little pins between my teeth while changing the doll's diaper and something happened. A pin disappeared. I looked everywhere and couldn't find it. I just knew I had swallowed it and would soon die. I went running to Mom and told her I thought I had swallowed a safety pin. I was about five at the time, and I wasn't ready to die. She told me I would know if I swallowed a pin. After much crying and begging to go to the doctor, she decided maybe it was a good idea to get an X-ray and see. No safety pin found. The ride home not so pleasant. Doctors cost money, what were you thinking, and the list goes on. Never did find that pin and I didn't die either, so it turned out good.

<u>Life Lessons</u>

Trust your decisions even if they end up seeming like a mistake
Think things through before doing what you've been told not to for your own good
Fight for what you believe is right and may be needed

_____
_____
_____
_____
_____
_____
_____
_____

"Really there are no mistakes, just opportunities to grow and sometimes it's hard."
~ Les Brown

Cold Water Down My Dad's Neck; Well He Said Prime the Pump

When my dad scolded me and booted my butt I was crushed.

"What I said Linda, is prime the pump, not pour water down the drain!" On the farm we didn't have running water, so there was a sink in the kitchen with a pump attached to it. We had to pump the handle to get water to come out. Once enough water was pumped out, we heated the water on the stove for washing dishes, taking baths, cleaning clothes, and everything we do today with our "running" hot water that comes out of the faucets. We were having a problem that night with the primer, and Dad was fixing it.

I was little, maybe five, and I didn't understand that when my Dad was under the sink, he was actually right under the drain. He wanted water poured into the top of the pump to prime it. Certain I thought I was helping my Dad, I poured a whole jar of cold water down the drain. He came flying out from under the sink mad as could be—and wet. Dad very rarely got mad so this scared me, and as I turned around, he gave me a boot to the butt. I tumbled, lost my balance, and slid to the floor. Did he boot my butt that hard? Maybe, maybe not. Yet with being scared and starting to run away, it felt hard and did cause me to slide and fall to the floor, crying of course. Soon he felt bad, and I was the one feeling mad. I didn't like it when my Dad hollered at me and punished me. I was embarrassed about what I had done, and the mistake I had made. He said, "How stupid are you anyway?" Nope, never have forgotten those words.

<u>Life Lessons</u>

We all have moments in life when we're not sure what we're supposed to do
Sometimes we know WHAT to do, do it, then find out that wasn't what was needed at all
When we find out our help wasn't what was needed, we usually feel bad enough about that.
Harsh words spoken usually stay with us—sometimes all our lives.

Before you speak out in anger or frustration, think about what you're saying and whether you want someone to carry those words the rest of their lives.

*"If you fall, fall on your back.
If you can look up, you can get up."*
~ Les Brown

The Day I Fell into the Flowing Creek

I had never been so cold and so sure that I was going to never see over the top of the iced-over water again.

My younger brother, older sister, and I did the thing we were told not to do. It was winter and where we lived there was a flowing creek with water six to seven feet deep. We were told to stay away from it many, many times. Well, it was a cold winter day, and we had our boots on and wanted to "skate" on the ice that was formed on the water. It was very frozen, we thought. My brother and sister went on first, and sure enough they were having great fun sliding around on the ice. They came off and said, "You should skate too, it's lots of fun." So I did. And, before they could get back on the ice, the ice cracked and I fell into the ice water.

Somehow I managed to grab the edge of the top of the crack with my mittens and they stuck. They froze to the ice, so I pulled myself up little by little.

The strength it took I should not have had as a little girl of six. I remember the freezing cold water hitting me, and I knew if my head went under I would never find that hole to come back up. It was very black. I hung on and cried and screamed and fought the pull of the water trying to drag me down. Finally, I made it to the top of the ice. A flowing creek can have quite an undercurrent, especially when it's fairly deep as this one was.

My brother and sister were in such shock they just stood there and couldn't help me, which is probably good, because with the weight with them on the cracked ice, we would all have fallen in. Once totally out of the water, we had to then make our way back to the house soaked and freezing over the quarter-mile walk.

All the way to the house I kept repeating my story, "I fell into a little puddle of water and got wet trying to get out; it was slippery." I may have said that 25 times out loud and was still repeating it when I walked into the house. My Mom saw me shivering so badly I could barely talk. She quickly got me out of my clothes deciding it was not the right time to scold me. We had a heater with doors that opened on either side for heat. She told me to stand by one side and keep turning around to warm up so I wouldn't get frostbite. It felt good, though itchy at the same time, which is sign of frostbite.

Once I was warmed up, the scolding started. "Now tell me," my Mom and Dad said at the same time. "What really happened?" When I came clean, they went white realizing how close to drowning I'd come. My Dad went down and checked the crack to see just how bad it was and how I managed to pull myself out, and maybe even to see if I was really telling the truth.

He came back and said there was a hole that went straight down, and he could see where my mitten must have caught on a rough edge allowing me to pull myself back up through the small opening.

I never got sick and never ice-skated again on that water. In fact, the near drowning gave me a fear of water which I carry with me to this day. It was very frightening, and I survived with my Angels' help I'm sure.

Life Lessons

Believe in a power greater than yourself
Fight for your life
Stay strong and get to where you need to go to be safe
Accept that some of life lessons come with consequences, and learn from them

_____
_____
_____
_____
_____
_____
_____
_____

"Life does not have to be so serious a lot of parts are funny try to find those parts."
~ linda nickey

Kids Say What They Hear

I thought the word was okay as I'd heard it all the time at home.

Many times we would go into our little rural town on Saturday evening to pick up groceries. I would usually go with Mom and my sister went with Dad—that's just the way it worked. I had heard the word "fart" used around our house often, so I didn't know it was only an at-home word.

My Mom was about to pay for the groceries, so she set me up on the counter. I was maybe four by then. As she was paying the bill, my Dad and sister walked in the front door of the grocery store. With my legs crossed sitting on the counter in a ho-hum waiting mode, I called out loud enough for everyone in the store to hear me say, "And where have you two little farts been?" My Mom was mortified and jerked me off my perch, yet not before I could see her smother a smile. So I thought, no spanking, it's all good. Off to get some ice cream, the treat for being good girls. Besides, I was little, I'd heard the word said often, and I really didn't know it was impolite/bad! ☺

<u>Life Lessons</u>

It's good to understand what's appropriate
and what's not
Lighten up and enjoy the moment
Words are important; use the ones you wouldn't mind
hearing in public from others quoting you

_____
_____
_____
_____
_____
_____
_____

"Forgive those who have hurt you."
~ Les Brown

Hair Pulled Right Out of My Head

Being scalped is not good.

My sister and I were playing "jump on the bed, flop down, and bounce". We knew we weren't supposed to do that. Mom had told us many times not too...yet it was fun. Once we were done jumping, we liked to hang on the bedpost upside down and would soon feel dizzy. Then we'd be back up for more jumping. So, as we merrily jumped up and down thinking we weren't going to get caught...then...we heard the sound of footsteps coming upstairs. Oh boy! She started to come up just as we were hanging from the bedpost. My sister jumped off first, and I started to come up not knowing she was standing on my hair. I had no choice. I had to get off that bedpost, and out came a handful of hair. We quickly grabbed it and threw it in the wastebasket by the bed. Now, all this happened in a quick minute. By the time Mom got there, we did our best to have innocent looks on our faces, even in the midst of my head feeling like it was about to fall off. No punishment, we didn't get caught, wheeeee, we thought! No, not so. A few days later, Mom brought down a handful of hair and said, "What happened here???" We came clean and dealt with the punishment, yet we knew we would try it again when we could. We were kids playing after all.

Life Lessons

Sometimes it's good to be quiet in spite of the pain
There's a benefit of sticking together
when in the "muck" together
Keep your sense of humor in the midst of it all

_____
_____
_____
_____
_____
_____
_____

"Life takes on meaning when you become motivated, set goals and charge after them in an unstoppable manner."
~ Les Brown

We Had to Beat the Rainstorm

Please dear God, don't let it rain.

My Dad and I had just stacked a load of hay very high up in his truck. We were having a contest to see how far I could reach the bale up towards him and how far down he could reach so we could make the load really high. I would put the bale on my knee, then lift it up to my shoulder to balance, and he would use a hook to pull the bale up and throw it on top of the stack. Finally, on the way home with our huge stacked load, we hit an approach at an odd angle and down they all came. We weren't happy, especially since we were trying to get the bales back to our farm before the coming rainstorm. We had to go to level ground in the field to do it all over again. I was about 10 then, and it was very hard work. Luckily I was so strong. It was almost always fun to help my Dad, even when it was hard work.

We laughed about it after awhile, well quite awhile. Maybe too long, because, you see it was about 9:00 pm, and our goal was still to beat the rainstorm coming in. We didn't want the bales in the field getting soaked and we had to get them back to the farm. We did beat the storm, just not the way we expected, having to load the same bails twice.

<u>Life Lessons</u>

Determination channels your energy
It's important to plan a goal to work towards
Keep a sense of humor
Be strong
Do what it takes to help

_____
_____
_____
_____
_____
_____
_____
_____

"Life has no limitations, except the ones you make."
~ Les Brown

Chores and Rewards

It's too early to get up!

It was a sunny morning and a freezing 10 below zero. Time to get up—there were chores to do before heading to school. The goal was to put on enough clothes to stay warm, which included a hat on my head and a scarf over it. The barn was always warmer with all the cows in there, and the smell—well powerful! Not only did I want to stay warm, but the smell of the barn was one I didn't want to carry with me for the day! Just no way for a girl to smell.

Being a farm girl, there were always chores to do. That's the way it was. We did the parts we could to be helpers. With a family of five kids of all ages, each of us did different chores. Work simply had to get done. Besides I got to be with my Dad when I was doing those chores, and I liked that. Even though the work was hard, we found things to laugh and joke about.

What I loved the most were the rewards for helping. I got to do things like driving the tractor when I was only eight. My Dad trained me by standing on the runner in case I had problems. The runner was between the seat of the tractor and the wheel, so he was close by. We were trained at a young age so we were prepared when needed.

It was fun and scary at times, too. I hardly ever drove over stuff I wasn't suppose to like hay bales, rakes, grassy areas, the garden—oh and sometimes a five-gallon milk can. I was so short, it was hard to reach the clutch and gas at the same time and also be able to brake. Just let me say, it was very hard! I did my best and sometimes it was funny—no real harm done.

Life Lessons

Do the best you can
Enjoy the process of learning
When you're part of a team to get things done,
do your part
Being scared is okay; sometimes
you need attention right then

Nana Says! Everything I Know I Learned On The Farm

> *"What did I learn that day…my fear was based on possibilities not actuality."*
> ~ Les Brown

Picking Rocks and the Unbelievable Happened

Did I bump her so she fell off? Thump, thump, and a load of rocks!

"Get to the back of the trailer!" That was our instruction, always. You see the trailer was full of rocks, and weighed maybe one ton or more—not sure. And it was being pulled by our tractor. We had to unload the rocks onto the rock pile about a mile away. We were told to sit in the back of the trailer, and because we liked to drag our feet through the alfalfa and play a game, we did as we were told. I think we may have been around seven and eight.

The minute my Dad got on the tractor and turned around, my sister and I ran to the front of the trailer, legs dangling. All of a sudden there was a bump, then another. My Dad turned around and looked at me and said, "Where's your sister?" I said, "She fell off," and he said, "My God, I think I ran over her."

It had all happened so fast, I just knew those thumps were my sister and she was probably dead. My Dad brought the tractor to a halt quickly. I went to the back of the trailer loaded with rocks to see if it was my sister. I jumped off, and sure enough, there she was, face down in the soil. Dad reached down and grabbed her asking, "Are you alright?" Her face was covered with dirt, as were her eyes. I went crazy screaming, "She's blind, she's blind!" Well that's what I thought with all the dirt in her face, eyes, and hair. I started to cry, in part because I thought she was blind, in part because she got up and was alive. My Dad said, "Stop screaming, Linda. She's not blind." Finally, he turned his full attention to my sister. She said she was okay, nothing hurt, and she could see. I was so happy she seemed okay.

My Mom was on the way out to the field with lunch, so we walked to where she was driving in. Of course, the way we all looked would have scared anyone and certainly not good for a woman nearly nine months pregnant and about to have our little brother. Mom rushed to town to the doctor, he took an x-ray of my sister and found nothing wrong. She was fine; she was swollen yet fine. Now, how can that be??? It was a load of rocks.

Five kids and never a broken bone and never any health insurance. Talk about living in risk! There was NO money for insurance and certainly no way to pay if we broke anything or ended up in the hospital, so none of us five kids ever did, ever!!

My grandparents were coming over for dinner later that day, and we wondered what they would say when they heard the story about my sister's accident. They took one look at her shiny red forehead and asked what happened. When repeated, the story sounded even worse, and I cried again. I thought it was my fault; it must have been because we were sitting side by side swinging our legs the same way and I didn't fall. I should have been able to hold onto her so she wouldn't fall.

Life Lessons

Not all bad things that happen are your fault
Sometimes when things work out well we may want to simply appreciate them and not guess why
When someone we trust asks us to not do something even when we don't understand,
It's good to listen and then decide

Nana Says! Everything I Know I Learned On The Farm

> *"Help others achieve their dreams and
> you will achieve yours."*
> ~ Les Brown

Future Homemakers of America (FHA) and Future Farmers of America (FFA)

I didn't like sewing aprons; bring me a calf to train.

Girls had to get special permission to be in FFA because it was considered a "boys" club, while homemaking was a girls club. Guess what? I was in both. I spent as much time outside helping my Dad—maybe more than inside doing family chores like laundry, scrubbing, dusting, cooking, cleaning, and more. In the boys club I had a calf to take care of—feed, walk, groom, and get fat for market (getting ready for sale).

It was very likely on any given afternoon when it was nice enough, I would put a rope around my calf's neck and teach her to walk with me as I commanded. On sunnier days I would bring out the bucket, wash her down, then brush her until her hair was shining. The goal: the better the calf behaved for the walk around the market barn, the better she looked, and the plumper she was, the better price we got when she was sold. People came to find the best of the best and FFA calves seemed to go for the highest price. That was good for us owners and good for the person buying the calf. It provided plenty of meat for their families since they bought them to slaughter for food. It sounds harsh, yet it was beef, and when managing a farm beef relates to food/meat and money.

Only once was I sad as I marched my very shiny calf around the market barn. I had become attached to her and now she had to be sold. I knew this when I started. Simply said, I felt like I was letting my loyal, obedient calf down. And, I really didn't want to keep her another year. I wanted a new calf to take care for the next year. It was what we did as Future Farmers of America; it was the business.

I liked learning about the business, listening to the stock market on the radio with my Dad to hear if prices were up or down and if it would be a good day for selling or buying. My calves seemed to always bring in a good price. I was asked often, "Do you get to keep the money?" No, I didn't nor did I expect too; this was part of the farm income and farm business. I was simply in FFA to learn and grow.

Life Lessons

Rules can be changed; they are simply rules
Work for what you want; take a stand
Hard work pays off
Know what you're doing and others can't take you off track; have a plan
Life is a team effort, so be a part of the team and do your part

_____
_____
_____
_____
_____
_____
_____
_____

"Character may be manifested in great moments, but it is made in the small ones."
~ Les Brown

My Younger Siblings Arrive

Kids everywhere! What a fun time!

My youngest brother is eight years younger and my sister nine years younger than me. My younger brother and sister were best friends, born about 18 months apart. They were both very cute babies born with dark hair and smooth, soft, peachy skin. I remember when they came home from the hospital. I was very excited and a bit awestruck. They were so little, and I seemed so big by comparison at eight years of age.

My little sister was born with the cord around her neck. Mom went into labor in the evening and hadn't delivered by night, so the doctor told the nurse to give Mom a sleeping pill and he would be back in the morning. If the delivery had been delayed much longer it could have been fatal. My sister's color already showed signs of air being cut off and she wasn't able to breathe right.

She did well in the hospital, though, and came home a few days later. Now, with two little people in the house, it surely changed the dynamics and responsibilities of us older kids. Soon, my older sister and I were changing diapers, feeding babies, and helping with the diaper laundry as Mom had things she did outside to help Dad with farm work. That's the way it was on the farm.

Our small kitchen now needed a high chair for my brother and a lap for my sister. It was fun to have the babies around, and they were amusing to watch as they grew from tiny infant to toddler. I believe my brother started walking in a bit less than a year. Of course my older sister and I coaxed him along the way with arms held out to see if he would take a step or two. He always had a runny nose it seemed and would smile in a way to help keep the moisture in; it was very cute and messy as it ran down to his upper lip.

We had a swivel chair, and as my sister grew to about six months, we would put both of them in the chair and twirl it around. Not when Mom was around since she wouldn't like that. It was during our babysitting times. The kids laughed and loved it. It wasn't too long before my brother found a way to crawl up on the chair and start to whimper for his sister to join him. She was only crawling at this time and required a little help from us bigger kids to get in the chair.

They also liked to crawl up the stair steps to the second floor for fun. It was all good until one of them would tumble down backwards—not hurt, just scared—and soon they would be off again. When it got too dangerous, we would close the door to the upstairs which they found quite annoying and demonstrated their frustration with crying. If one cried the other did...like twins.

Is he breathing?

Before my sister was born, I would always beg to hold my brother on my lap on the way to church. We were in the back seat (no seat belts as that time). He seemed to fall asleep on the ride and my Mom loved that. He was so sound asleep, he would sometimes sleep all through church. One Sunday he fell asleep so fast and I couldn't feel his breathing—which I usually could. It scared me, so I tried to move him around. Still no sounds. Pretty soon I decide to squeeze his arm a bit to see if he would move. He got so startled, he let out a cry and cried for the next five minutes.

Mom wasn't happy and asked me what happened. I said, "I don't know. He just woke up crying." To be honest, I was happy. At least I knew he was alive!! I wasn't always offered to hold him after that. I didn't like it, because he was fun to hold and rock on my lap.

Where to sleep

We had three bedrooms upstairs in our farm home. First my youngest brother was in the nursery where his crib fit just fine. Then when my baby sister came along the sleeping situation had to change. The room was too small for two cribs, although we did have two beds in the room for a while: a bassinette and a crib. Once my younger brother was two, he moved into the bedroom where his big brother had a double bed. My little sister now had the crib and the room to herself like a private nursery. That lasted for a period of time, yet she didn't seem to like it much.

Once she was old enough, she found her way out of crib in the middle of the night. She crawled down two flights of steps and fell asleep on the couch where we found her in the morning. She may have been about one at the time. After trying to put her to bed in her crib several nights in a row only to find her downstairs each morning, the family made a decision. We would make the couch her sleeping quarters. We made up the couch bed each night lining the front of it with chairs so she wouldn't roll off. That became her new bed. My other sister and I shared a room, and there was no room for another bed. Once my little sister became the night crawler, our options were limited. The couch was her bed for years, and she talks about it often to this day. Somehow it became the norm, and we didn't think it was so unusual, since she seemed to like it. Knowing the alternative of having her crawl around at night with the high potential to fall down one or two flights of steps, the couch seemed like a good idea.

What did happen that day when driving our pickup?

When my little sister was about three, she was with me in the pickup standing on the passenger side of the seat. I'm not sure if we were taking lunch out to the field where Mom and Dad were working or if we had an errand to run in town. At any rate, I was maybe 12 and still had trouble touching the gas pedal and clutch at the same time for shifting. As we were leaving the yard, I'm not sure if I was going too fast or if the clutch slipped. Whatever it was, I hit a big bump in the dirt road, the glove box flew open, and my sister fell into the corner of it and cut her arm open. I got so scared! I was kind of mean and told her to quit crying—and more I'm sure. It was pretty bad and bleeding a lot, and she continued to cry. I was too young to have good judgment about what to do so I got mad. It seemed to cover up my fear that I knew she was hurt and it was my fault. To this day I feel bad about that and wish it hadn't happened. It must have hurt pretty bad for sure, and I didn't do a good job of taking care of her when she was in pain. I really just didn't know what to do.

What were you thinking?

The quick answer would be, "I don't know," followed by "I wasn't thinking." My oldest brother, four at the time, was playing catch with my Dad in the front yard. My Dad had to go into the house for a minute. Soon my brother found a old corncob which may have been in the yard for weeks drying up. It had sharp thistles where the corn kernels used to be. He started kicking it around playing his own game while waiting for us.

When my Dad came out of the house, he said, "Let's play ball; throw me the ball." Without thinking, my brother quickly picked up the corncob and flung it as hard and high as he could. It hit my Dad right in the eye. It all went very fast. My dad screamed, "What the heck were you thinking? That wasn't the ball." With that, my Dad went running into the house, pumped some water, and started washing his eye out as quickly as he could. When he came back outside, his eye was red and looked swollen. He took one look at my little brother and could see he had scared the daylights out of him with that scream so he didn't punish him further. It was an accident. A painful one, yet an accident.

Life Lessons

Change even when good can be hard
Enjoy the moments, and know they make good memories in spite of what they may seem
When you're wrong say you're sorry and know it's okay to move on when you've done the best you can
Sometimes we're too young for the responsibility given to us
Laughing helps lighten the load

Do your best and know it's the best you could do

"*Happiness is wanting what you have,
even when change is involved.
Find the fun and flow with the change.*"
~ linda nickey

"Well, it is said that what we do after we make a mistake is more important than the original error."
~ Les Brown

Do Not Go in the Chicken Coop

I hated the chicken coop yet found myself inside, stuck.

I didn't like picking eggs. Going in the chicken coop was smelly, damp, and the chickens were always clucking making so much noise it was hard to hear. Once in the chicken coop one of two things was about to happen: I was either going to reach under the clucking hens to get eggs and be pecked at, or I was there with a rake to clean out the damp, smelly hay, the waste dump for the hens. Yuck, yuck, yuck! They were both worse than slopping the pigs or hauling manure!!

One day, my Dad and Grandpa were taking a chicken coop off the property or bringing it on—I just don't remember which. I was about eight. The chicken coop was sitting in the middle of the farmyard with the door wide open, and there were several windows around the side. Dad and Grandpa headed to the barn with one last warning. "Don't go in the chicken coop. The door will swing shut, and you may not be able to get out."

Kids being kids, it was maybe a minute that they were out of sight and in I went. I heard the door slam as it swung shut. I thought it had locked! Of course, I was within earshot of my Dad, yet my scream came right along with my fist through the window. I had to get out of the stinky hot coop. My Dad came running. Seeing that I was alright, he started scolding and I started crying. I could have opened the door, I was told. That's not what I heard when he had said, "The door will shut and you may not be able to get out." To me that meant I was locked in and about to suffocate from the smell of wet hay and hen poop. And that was not about to happen. I didn't understand the door only locked from the inside and that I simply had to turn the handle to get out. I had panicked.

I remember how hard I hit that window to break it, yet I had no cuts, no bruises, just a broken window, and a very upset Dad. This story was retold so many times, and each time it seemed to give everyone a good laugh, well except me. I didn't find funny at all.

Life Lessons

*It's a good idea to listen and do as told
when there's good reason to
Before trying hard solutions, try the easier ones
Some things that seem very difficult may not be,
so check all options
Do not panic, breathe, think, then act
There's almost always someone available to help in
difficult times, and not far away
If it's funny, laugh with others even if at your own
expense, because it just may be funny*

_____
_____
_____
_____
_____
_____
_____
_____

> *"Honor your commitments with integrity."*
> ~ Les Brown

Singing Well, Not So Much

How could I get talked into singing? I can't sing.

My older sister and I were asked to sing "Jesus Loves Me" at my Grandma's "church ladies group". We didn't sing in front of people, only with our dolls. Of course Mom could hear us. I guess we may have been about five and six—very little, so everything looked cute to others. The invite came and Mom really wanted us to sing, so we all went to the ladies meeting and the tummy nerves were upon us! There must have been 30 ladies there waiting for us to sing. We took it very seriously and didn't know then that no matter how we sounded, we would be a hit.

So up we went as they introduced us and started to sing the song. Pretty soon, my sister was crying, so I started to cry. We looked up, and now Mom was crying. We were all a mess. The ladies tried to console us, yet we were embarrassed for Mom and Grandma. We didn't ever want to sing in public again. No way! Yet after the meeting, there were cookies, brownies, soft drinks, and coffee, with compliments flowing from all the ladies. But, we still felt bad.

How sad really that we got embarrassed and felt bad. Singing was fun for my sister and me to do together at home. We should have kept it that way. We still sang to our dolls in our make believe church on the steps. That we liked a lot.

Life Lessons

Following the leader is not always best;
pay attention to your own instincts
Be brave in tough situations; just do your best
and try to enjoy the moment
Family is very important
Many times we put pressure on ourselves
way beyond what anyone else puts on us
When embarrassed just know it will pass and usually
it's not as bad as you think

Nana Says! Everything I Know I Learned On The Farm

_____
_____
_____
_____
_____
_____
_____
_____

"All of us need to grow continuously in our lives."
~ Les Brown

Surprise Birthday Party and Little Brother Swinging Out of Hayloft Door

Never knew how high up the barn loft looked until my brother came flying out of it.

My sister and I had our first surprise birthday party ever when we were eight and nine. Besides a few of our friends, my parents also invited a few of their friends, and it was fun. My sister got so excited with one of her gifts that when she cut open the package, she cut right through the part of a billfold that holds it together ruining the clasp. The gift was ruined and she felt very bad. The lady who gave it to her said all the right things and we got past it, just in time for another incident.

We looked up to see my little brother swinging out the upstairs barn door loft on a rope. At the time he was five. As he flew out the barn door, he looked like he was having a good time, laughing and happy. He then let go of the rope and down he came. My Dad went running out to check on him. He found him stunned yet not hurt, no broken bones, thank goodness. Again, remember we didn't have any insurance, so no accidents allowed!!

The day ended with lots of fun, some fear, and many gifts. There was a little scolding for my sister with her rush to open her gift. My brother was scolded for going into the loft of the barn and then jumping. He was told he wasn't ever to do that again!! I'm pretty sure they wouldn't have had to tell him that, as he was very scared; it was quite a fall for a little guy.

Life Lessons

Take your time
When life is threatened, nothing else matters
Have fun and laugh at your mistakes,
and others will too

"Anytime you suffer a setback or disappointment, put your head down and plow ahead."
~ Les Brown

Changing Schools Was Hard Work

I didn't like my new school. Not at all.

I went to a small one-room schoolhouse with grades one through eight. When I was in first grade, a new school was completed with a full basement for lunch and some of the classes. Each older classmate helped the teacher with the younger students by listening to their reading, and sometimes with other subjects as well. I wasn't a good reader and could have used some one-on-one time with the teacher. That wasn't the way it was in a small school of 17 kids and all eight grades.

When I was going into the third grade, we moved from one farm to another and I had to change schools. It was hard to go to a school where there were so many students in my class. In the old school, it was one other girl and me. The new school had 20 or more and there were a few grades together. I was no longer in the classroom my sister was in, and that made me sad. I didn't like it at all! I wasn't a very good student and I was shy. Being in a big class and feeling not as smart as most wasn't fun. The teacher wasn't sympathetic. It made her job harder, I guess, to take time to help me with so many students. I always did my best which didn't seen like enough to my teacher. I never felt that she liked me or wanted to help me.

Grandpa died—so many changes so fast

While going to this new school, my Grandpa died unexpectedly at quite a young age of 64. He fell off a tractor and hit his head on the tongue between the tractor and the piece of farm equipment he was pulling. The doctor said he had a heart attack, then fell off, and the blow to his head is what caused his death. It was a shock!

Grandpa had in his will that he wanted my Mom, his daughter, and my Dad to buy and run the farm when he passed away. Grandma was only 57 and she didn't want to be on the farm alone. So, in a short time we moved onto the family farm that had been Grandpa's and Grandma's. It all seemed to go really fast. It was a time of much confusion and lots of sadness.

When we moved to Grandpa's farm, we were back to my old school district. I was happy about that. I had gone almost a year to the big school in town, which with 75 or more students felt big to me. It was too different and I had trouble adjusting.

Moving was fun. Of course at 10 there weren't too many responsibilities that came with a move. The farm chores were the same wherever we lived: cows, pigs, chickens, crops to harvest, a garden to plant, and so on. Grandpa's farm was modern and so nice. We had running water and an indoor toilet—luxuries for us after pumping water and having outhouse toilets.

We had a furnace that heat came out of from the floor, not a stove in the middle of the room to heat the whole house. The heat would even go up to the bedrooms if we left the doors open, so there was heat in the winter in the bedrooms, which was very nice.

We were all so sad that Grandpa passed away, and it was a very difficult time. Grandma lived with us for awhile, then she stayed a short time with each of her other four kids until they could all build her a home in town by the church. Grandma never drove, so it was important she had a place close to her church, with friends and a grocery store close by. She had relied on Grandpa for everything. It was very hard for her for years to learn to live without him and to care for herself. Her five children did all they could to help take care of her; they wanted to make her life as easy as possible, since she was so unhappy.

Everyone had lots of change to work through and get used too. Living on the family farm with what we considered luxury had its problems. So remembering these times stirs lots of memories.

This story may sound a little mixed up and that's exactly the way I felt that whole time. Lots of conversations I didn't understand, plenty of arguments, much upheaval, and my first time of seeing someone I loved pass away. Many times I felt scared along with sad. I was unsure of many things. I don't remember having much comfort during this time; other people and things took priority, and there was much to get done.

Life Lessons

Change is often hard and takes time to adjust to
The familiar feels good and yet one must grow
Loss is painful
Seeing people sad is hard and there's
a helpless feeling for most of us
Family takes care of family whatever
your "family" is to you
Love is good and love is hard

_____
_____
_____
_____
_____
_____
_____
_____

"You live then you die and there's a lot
that goes on between the two."
~ linda nickey

> *"I advise you to say your dream is possible and then overcome all inconveniences, ignore all the hassles and take a running leap through the hoop, even if it is in flames."*
> ~ Les Brown

Babysitting: Didn't Like It, No Did Not

Didn't like to babysit; let me milk cows instead.

My two younger siblings were eight and nine years younger than me and another brother was three years younger. This meant my older sister and I were their babysitters often. No one trained us for the job; it was just a given that we older kids would watch over the younger kids. I didn't mind it, although sometimes it was very hard and I didn't always make the best choices. I scolded them, since that's what I heard from my parents, so it seemed right. Yet it usually meant tears for one of the kids—not good—and I felt bad often. Many times I simply didn't know what to do. How do you know how to parent when you're 10 years of age? You just do the best you can.

When neighbors wanted me to babysit at 10, they knew I was well trained. I really didn't want to, yet my

Mom thought it was a good idea. We lived 10 miles from the big town of 4,500 people, so where I babysat was very rural. All the natural critter noises were scary to me, and I knew I was responsible as the sitter for these kids I was watching over.

One time, and only one time, did I babysit for this family with four kids. I was picked up by the parents because we lived three miles away. Once inside their home, they announced that a couple of friends were bringing their kids over too, so it would be more fun for the kids. I ended up with 10 kids under the age of eight.

It was the norm that when parents went out, they prepared dinner for the kids. My job and expectation was to feed them, wash the dishes, and prepare their bedtime snack which was always a special treat because the parents were out. Things like ice cream floats, popcorn, chips and dip, and pop. Then I had to clean up after that as well. I hated it all, in fact I didn't even like the kids. It was noisy, they were hard to manage, and difficult to get into bed. It just seemed like more of what I already did at home. I was happier cleaning windows and peeling five-pound bags of potatoes for the neighbors.

After three babysitting jobs, I said no more. At the last babysitting job I did with these combined families, they paid me five dollar for the night. They were out until 2:00 am and I started at 7:00 pm. The next day my Mom and I drove over and I had to tell them they paid me too much and give two dollars back. Mom didn't want us to look greedy to the neighbors.

I hated that night; it was horrible at best. The worst part was at the end of the night when the Dad had to give me a ride home. He usually seemed to me like he had a bit too much to drink and was very chatty—yuk!

So from then on I babysat my siblings and no others. I cleaned houses and did other money-making things, but no outside babysitting jobs for me. None!

Life Lessons

It's important to try things and see if it works for you;
if not move on
Not everything we do will be fun and yet it
may be a way to grow and learn
Know your worth and stand tall in it
You don't have to be good everything;
learn from what doesn't work and move on

_____
_____
_____
_____
_____
_____
_____
_____

"Lighten up and enjoy all the rides of your life."
~ linda nickey

Roller Skating and Playing "Crack the Whip"; Not Good to Be on the End

Flying on roller skates, knee pads please.

Roller skating was tons of fun. Some of our outings for special school events included going into the big town of 4,500 people and skating at Funland. Parents took turns driving us to town and staying while we skated. I was about 10 at the time and found skating so much fun! We had someone help us with our roller skate rental size to get us up and skating. None of us had any fear. If we fell, so what? We got right back up and started again.

Sometimes they called out different type of skates where girls asked the boys. Sometimes they had someone pick a particular kind of skating, like a waltz, two-step, jitterbug, and so on. Of course we wanted fast music which was the most energizing and exciting.

One day, we talked the manager into letting us play crack the whip, which meant we all held hands. Someone was the leader and started skating doing circles, cutting across the rink and so on. One time I happened to be on the end of the whip, where we had about 20 kids holding hands and building momentum. Then it happened. I went so fast. The leader turned a sharp circle and I went flying off. I fell on my right knee and skidded across the rink floor leaving a stream of blood. One of the managers came and rescued me. I could barely stand and felt kind of sick. I was in a lot of pain and trying not to cry. I wasn't sure I wanted to see my knee. Once I was sat down, the manager brought over the first aid kit. I could see the skin on my knee was gone and blood was running down my white bobby socks. My goal was: do not cry, get my knee bandaged, and get back to skating. It took about 20 minutes to get all the blood off the floor of the rink.

Then the manager called "all skate" and he and I went onto the floor leading the skate doing a two-step to a round of applause. I wasn't going to have my happy skating time cut short as it happened way too seldom. I loved skating, and even though my knee hurt, I skated! I was very grateful nothing was broken. Remember, no insurance!!

A little cool tidbit: the manager who helped me out that night became my boyfriend a few years later.

He was an awesome skater and he taught me how to dance on skates. I loved the free feeling of going fast around the rink and doing many fun turns forward backward and in circles.

A happy memory.

Life Lessons

Having fun can cure a lot of pain
Play and laugh often; it's healing
Be a team player even if it's risky at times

_____
_____
_____
_____
_____
_____
_____
_____

"One thing for sure, today will not be any better than your thoughts; choose wisely."
~ linda nickey

Lunch in the One-Room Schoolhouse

I prefer my food without feathers in it.

Here's how lunch worked for us in the one-room schoolhouse. It was based on the number of kids in the school; the more kids, the faster your rotation came up. We had about six or seven families that made up our 17 to 20 students. If you had three children in school, it became a quicker rotation than those with one or two. That's just the way it was set up. We did get some school commodities like rice, beans, milk, and sometimes Delicious apples from Washington State—a great day at the school!

The Moms did their best to make lunches "all" the kids would eat, including one or two loaves of old home white bread just in case we didn't eat the food. One family didn't do so well. We could look at the rotation and see when this family's turn was coming up. It was an, "Oh no!!" We knew it meant canned pork and beans, white bread, and it usually included a bit of straw, hay, feather, or other item not meant to be in the bean dish.

The family kept a very messy farm along with unclean selves, so this was just part of the way it was. They didn't mean harm; it was the way they lived their life, and we were a part of it with the school lunch food rotation program. It wasn't nice to complain, as the Moms worked hard to make the food. They then delivered the food, picked up the remains at the end of the day, took home the dirty dishes, and washed them only to know in four or five days they would be doing the same thing.

The families decided they wanted us kids to have a "hot" lunch rather than each Mom pack a lunch for their kids. I believe this hot lunch rotation went on for two to three years before we all ended up with brown bags or lunch pails. We kids were happy about that, and I think the Moms were too. It was a big job to feed 17 to 20 kids lunch once a week!

Life Lessons

Be gracious
Do your part
Help when needed
Be kind and do what's right, not easy right

> *"Confront the difficult while it is easy,*
> *accomplish the great one step at a time."*
> ~ Chinese Proverb

Dad Liked to Tease Me

It's hard to think funny when you're at the brunt of a bad joke.

I was waiting for a certain special boy to call me in hopes that he would ask me for a date. I was 15. I'd been wandering around the house hopeful that whenever the phone rang it would be for me—and to no avail. We had a party line, so our time on the phone was always very limited and could be easily dropped in on by anyone on our party line. I didn't like that.

Well when the phone finally rang, my Dad called, "Oh llllliiiinnnddda, it's for you." I was upstairs, so I came flying down the steps. That's when he knew he had taken a prank too far. The excited happy look on my face seen by my dad was only to be followed by, "There was no call for you. I was just teasing." Well I cried, and my feelings were very hurt that he would be so mean. Once he knew how upset I was, he apologized. But it didn't help either!! It was a mean thing to do, and I was mad at him. The boy never did call that day; however, he did call another time, so that made me happy.

Life Lessons

Teasing can go too far and then it's painful
Be clear on your expectations
Crying is the best answer sometimes;
do so boldly; it's healing
It's okay to get angry; say why and tell the person what they did was hurtful

_____
_____
_____
_____
_____
_____
_____
_____

TWO:

The Tween Years—

A

Confusing and Chaotic Time

"I advise you to say your dream is possible and then overcome all inconveniences, ignore all hassle and take a running leap through the hoop, even if it is in flames."

~ Les Brown

The "Tween" Years Were a Hectic, Confusing Time for Me

As I look back on the years 10 through 14, I realize there were many changes. All the days and years run together. It was a very busy, hectic time.

I was 10 at the time we moved onto Grandpa's farm about six months after his passing. When we moved, my Mom was pregnant with my youngest sister and my youngest brother was one. The family dynamics changed and we now were a family with five children—baby up to 11 years old.

My sister and I helped a lot with caring for our younger siblings. We babysat all three of them often when my parents were getting our new farm and home in order. When I could, I helped with outside chores. My oldest brother was only seven and my older sister was struggling with asthma, so I was it, and I didn't mind.

There was no time to put things on hold or slow down. The crops had to be cared for, the cows had to be milked, school was about to start, we were going back to our "old" school, my Grandma was living with us part-time, and our family chaos mounted.

Along with moving to the family farm, there were many sibling fights among my Mom's family. Some of the siblings didn't like that my Dad was the person my Grandpa wanted to buy the farm. They thought it should have been one of them even though they each had their own farms or other work life they were involved in. My Dad and Mom were the only ones at that time still renting farmland and a farm home. It made sense, yet emotions ran strong. My parents often fought about this and it wasn't good.

Living on a farm with running water, an indoor toilet, four bedrooms (the very small one was used as a nursery), and big dining/living room were all very positive. We even had a basement and a crawl space for vegetables and canned goods. In the midst of all the good things going on, the stress level was high. It wasn't easy being the son-in-law now running the family farm.

There were new costs added to the family budget. My older sister was being treated for asthma. My baby sister needed baby shots and the things required for infants. There was farm equipment to buy, a bigger car was needed, and we even had to rent a bull to breed the cows.

To add to the cost, my Mom was set on my sister and me taking piano lessons. I'm not sure if we bought the piano or if it was left with the house. I remember Grandpa playing a piano. He also played the violin. All I knew was that it was VERY important to Mom that we take lessons. But, I hated it! As much as she wanted us to take lessons, the cost of them were brought up each time we had a lesson. There was no fun in it for me. My sister liked it and was quite good. I think I may have stayed in the same lesson book the whole time I took lessons!! I wasn't enjoying any part of it.

When Grandma was with us on the sibling rotation cycle (until her house was built in town), she would ask us to play. I was a disappointment to anyone listening— just the way it was. I preferred to go out and clean the barn, quite frankly. Playing the piano made me nervous. I was always hitting the wrong key and trying one more time to get it right.

When it was time to prepare for high school, I felt a bit of fear. The school seemed so big. There would be 100 plus in my class, my sister told me. I had just graduated from the eighth grade with one other girl. My grades weren't good, and I was scared of the unknown, though excited too. My sister at one year ahead of me was doing great. Her grades were awesome. She was very popular, well liked by everyone. I wanted to be just like her!

We had to ride with a boy who lived close by who was called a "hoodlum". He drove fast, he smoked, he wore shirts with the sleeves rolled up above his elbow, he wore his shirt collar up, he swore often—all signs of a "hoodlum" according to my parents, yet we needed a ride. He was nice enough. The only thing that scared my sister and me was the speed at which he drove, even on layered ice. My parents liked his parents, so we rode the 10 miles to school with him; options were limited.

High school seemed overwhelming to me at first, coming from a small rural school. Yet, I was liked and accepted, so I quickly adjusted. My grades suffered, however. I tried to get my studies done in study hall, but it was hard to do. Studying at home didn't work for me either as the noise level of seven people in the house made it seem chaotic most of the time. The fights between my parents were worsening.

I was eager to get a job and make my own money. My job cleaning the neighbors' house was gone, and there was more need for my help at home. I learned early on how important it was to me to be independent and have my "own" money. There were a lot of arguments between my parents about not having enough money. I wanted to do my part to help—get a job and work for money!

During my sophomore year I did get a job. I started to work as a nurse's aide. I was soon learning the value and importance of improving my grades so I could further my studies in nursing and hopefully get into college. I worked hard to do so, getting private one-on-one tutoring with one of my teachers. Two of my teachers took me under their wing to make sure I got through a couple of much needed classes for college. I was also fortunate that I had some smart friends to help me along the way as well

The fun times I recall are going to the stock car races, picnics at the dam, dinners with friends, getting popcorn when we went to town with Mom and Dad, watching my younger brothers and sister grow, drive-in movies with my grandparents, overnight stays with friends, learning to cook, and roller skating.

This has been the most difficult part of the book to write. Some of the memories I have of this time are very painful. I've decided the feelings I have about my negative family situations wouldn't add to my story. In fact, they may cause pain for others so I chose not to include a lot about those times.

Once I turned 15 and started work, my life began to change. I could see making a plan for college and moving was a real possibility. This thought became my focus. I loved my family, yet wanted to move on.

There was so much I wanted to accomplish, goals to meet, places to see, and adventures to experience. I needed a less chaotic environment. I wanted to live a bigger life and see a bigger world. I wanted to be challenged, grow, and expand beyond my local area.

As I prepared for this time, I made a plan to move out when I turned 18. And I did. You'll read a story about that later.

Life Lessons

Be strong in your beliefs
Find the parts you love and build on them
Most times a fight doesn't solve problems
Not everything that goes wrong in
relationships is your fault
It helps to stay positive in the midst of chaos
Look for the light at the end of the tunnel;
make a plan and have a goal

What are some of your "tween" memories?

_____
_____
_____
_____
_____
_____
_____
_____
_____
_____

THREE:

Memories

of the

Farm Fun Times

"If you are carrying strong feelings about something that happened in your past, they may hinder your ability to live in the present."
~ Les Brown

Some of My Fun Thoughts; I Like Remembering Them

• I liked to arm wrestle with Dad. He had big biceps and I thought if I could beat him I must be very strong. Now I am pretty sure at six, seven, eight, or even nine it wasn't going to happen. I decided I would involve my younger brother and/or older sister by asking them to help me. Still to no avail. He did "let" us slap his arm right down to the table a few times, usually when he knew from the force one of us was going to tumble to the floor as he quickly let go. We thought it was fun trying, and it made us all laugh.

• If my Dad wanted me to help with something and I was fighting it a bit, he would say, "I'll buy you an ice cream cone if you help." No matter what, I was going to help and he knew it, yet when he teased me with the promise of an ice cream cone which made it more fun. If I actually got all those promised ice cream cones, I would have weighed in at 300 pounds by 11. My Mom didn't like when he said that, because she knew I wasn't getting all those ice creams. I didn't care, because I liked when he said it; it was our little game. Even at age six, I knew this was a Dad game.

- I always wanted to do a good job when I helped around the house or in the barn, I liked when my Mom and Dad were happy with what I did to help. Chores in the house were a bit harder to get "atta girl" for because my Mom was a cleaning perfectionist. On the farm it was always dirty to some degree. Many times I was told to do it again—sweep, wipe down the counters, dust the furniture, and more. Hard to do it good enough.

- What made the barn chores easier was that I liked sweeping down the barn floor sending stuff into the gutter. My Dad would say, "You've cleaned that barn so good, it's shinier than a monkey's ass." Now I know that's not a nice word, yet it made me laugh and I knew he was pleased, and that's what I wanted to hear.

- Both my sister and I started to help with many chores by the age of five to six. We couldn't do a lot, yet the expectation was we did what we could. We helped with laundry as we had no automatic washer and dryer. We had a ringer washer in the basement and tubs to rinse the clothes in. We would stand on a cement block and put the clothes into the tubs, rinse them, and put them through the ringer several times to get some of the water out. Once ready for the clothes basket, we each took one side to carry the basket up the steps to Mom so she could hang the clothes on the clothesline.

- We had five-gallon milk cans that had to be taken down to the flowing well to be kept cold until the milkman arrived in the morning. Early on I learned that in order for me to do that job, I had to find a way to go back and forth with the can the 20 yards or so to get it lined up by the flowing well to be lifted in by my Dad.

- My sister and I played dolls a lot and Mom would help us with ideas. She saved fruit crates, and we used those for our "grocery" store shelves. Inside the crate shelves we put empty cans, bottles, and boxes—

whatever we could find to play store. We brought our crying misbehaving dolls with us when "shopping". This wasn't always so popular as they were very loud and sometimes they even got a spanking/swat for it. Usually when Mom said, "Quiet down with those kids of yours," we would. We would laugh sometimes, because we did make them almost seem real.

- We also took the dolls to "church" with us which we held on the steps going upstairs in our house. My sister and I couldn't really sing, yet we knew a few songs from Sunday school and we would belt them out loud and clear. My sister usually sat up towards the top of the steps, and I would be in the middle pretending it was a full crowd. Many times those dolls would have to be taken out to have their diapers changed, and we did this together; then we came right back to our church service to sing. We had fun doing that and really did "pretend" well. Most of our toys were dolls and a few dolls clothes, although we made things for them too. My younger brother had trucks and tractors. Sometimes he played make believe with us, and we liked that.

• My sister and I loved to go out to the water flowing through our property by the trees and play pretend, cooking, feeding our doll babies, building our house, making furniture with branches—we loved it all. Our favorite might have been making mud pies. We would get a tin can and mix dirt and water together to make the makeshift pie, then go to the barn and get some white ground feed and mix it up with water for a topping. We were very creative. We really didn't have a lot of toys, and I don't remember minding that. We used our creative minds to come up with "things" to do and games to play. Playing together was a lot of fun, and yes, the fights we had were sometimes not so good, yet we always made up.

• We had a very big farmyard with a huge yard post and a light at the top. We played many outside games. When the weather was nice we played Kick the Can, Blind Man's Bluff (inside or outside), ball-related games of catch, a game called 500, and Shot the Can off a post with a gun. Moonlight Starlight and Hide and Seek in the dark with lots of farm noises were spooky games. We would get scared sometimes and come out to get caught!

- We had tricycles too and would ride them around the yard down to the barn, chicken coop, and granary pretending we were on a very long trip. Of course once we out grew the trikes we made up other games to play, until quite a bit later when we got a bicycle to share.

- I actually was driving the tractor and pickup before I rode a bike. I started driving the tractor at eight and shortly thereafter the pickup with things propped behind me so I could reach both the clutch and the gas pedal at the same time. Now it seems amazing the trust it must have taken for my Dad to let me drive at such a young age. The answer very likely is that on the farm everyone started to help as early as they could. Hired hands were too expensive. It seemed natural to me. My brother was three years younger than me, so he couldn't help until later, and my older sister had very bad asthma and couldn't do some of the outside chores. If she did, she would get very ill.

What fond memories do you like to remember and talk about with family and friends?

_____
_____
_____
_____
_____
_____
_____
_____

"Life has no limitations, except ones we make."
~ Les Brown

As I remember many things I observed that didn't seem so big at the time, now I realize they were priceless experiences, each teaching me a lesson.

Following each statement I've written what I think may have been my life lesson and for others as well. You may want to write what you think the lesson may be, as there could be many different ones.

1. How baby chicks struggle to break out of the egg.
Lesson: If you try to hurry the birth along, they may likely die. We need the struggle to fully develop and prepare for life.

2. The humor of watching ducklings when they first try to walk.
Lesson: They spread their web feet for balance and many times simply fall down only to get up again to try. We can learn from them to get up when life knocks us down.

3. The difficulty cows can have when birthing their baby and the help they sometimes need.
Lesson: The sign language cows use for help can't go unnoticed. They're willing to accept the help and so should we.

4. Watching the big old pigs giving birth and finding many times they don't have much interest in their babies…until they're bigger.
Lesson: We put their babies in a cardboard box, brought them in the house, and set the box on the opened oven door to provide the little bit of warmth they needed to survive and live. It's the right thing to do to help the helpless—critters in this case!

5. When milking cows, it's interesting to see how far back they can kick; it's important to know how to get out of their way.
Lesson: Sometimes stepping back is the right and best way to handle a situation that could be unhealthy for us or even dangerous.

6. Chickens are very noisy when laying eggs and not very friendly.

Lesson: It's good to know that leaving those irritable chickens alone when they're doing important work is a good idea as they need uninterrupted time. Just like people.

7. How the big old bull dominates the scene when he arrives at the barnyard.
Lesson: Sometimes we have the "big old bulls" in our life, and they want to take over. It's good to set some boundaries and know what you want without compromising if it's not right for you. It's good to be strong.

8. Not knowing there should have been fear along with excitement as low flying airplanes flew overhead spraying for bugs. It did kill bugs after all.
Lesson: When we think there's danger, it's worth checking out the situation to learn what the dangers are. Maybe you need to be somewhere else and not a part of it.

9. How using a hand push lawn mower was made to be fun.
Lesson: Being a team player and getting someone to help push the mower made it more fun and easier. It's

okay to ask for help when needed, and not all work is fun, yet needs to be done.

10. Never did understand the purpose of pulling dandelions when they just came right back.
Lesson: Sometimes it's good to be doing something productive even if we don't understand why the particular job is important. It may just be a part of the whole process not yet seen or understood.

11. The feeling of accomplishment when washing the cars by hand always surprised me.
Lesson: Certainly praise for a job well done feels good. It was nice to ride in a clean well cared for vehicle. Most of the time pride in being helpful feels good and may make someone happy.

12. The never-ending job of shoveling snow during the winter was exhausting.
Lesson: Some jobs have to be done many times to stay on top of situations. It's good to be prepared for the "next" storm should it happen.

13. I could feel the benefit of shoveling coal into the basement furnace, as warmth came almost immediately.
Lesson: Some actions simply have immediate benefit; enjoy it and feel the joy of the reward.

14. There was value in pumping water from the hand pump into pails and then carrying them to the garden to water the vegetables.
Lesson: It's fun to watch the beauty of growth even when it takes time. Often there are many trips to the unknown before we see the beautiful end result. That's called faith.

15. How fun it was to pick corn and bring it home to have for dinner in just a few minutes.
Lesson: There's a beauty in planting the seed, tending the garden, watching the growth, and seeing in the end there's a rich, wonderful gift waiting for us.

16. Cleaning the outdoor toilets was just part of the chores and not a fun job. I did it anyway as part of the family team and in as good a spirit as I could muster up. Part of the cleaning was that we used Lysol and the smell gave me a headache. Yet when they were

clean it certainly made it much more pleasant for everyone to use the "facility".

Lesson: Sometimes we simply have to do what needs to be done even if we don't like it.

17. Somehow Grandpa made saddling up the horses to go out and plow the field look like fun. For me it seemed frightening, as the horses were huge. When I saw him managing the horses as he plowed through fields, he looked happy to me and I liked that.

Lesson: Even at times, some things that are hard or hard work, can be fun and rewarding.

18. When my Grandma broke her wrist on Thanksgiving eve day, had a cast put on, and then continued to make the family dinner. We arrived to see Grandma carrying a pot of potatoes with two hands. She wasn't going to give up no matter what. Grandpa was there helping her, and he assured us she didn't want anyone to know for fear someone might take over one of her favorite holidays. Her joy was to cook Thanksgiving dinner for her family and include homemade rye bread, rice pudding, homemade butter for the potatoes, and many other Swedish dishes.

Lesson: Family traditions are important. It may even mean we have to tough it out and do the best we can when challenges come up so we don't break a longtime tradition.

19. One day we arrived at Grandma's, my Mom's Mom when we were very little. Grandma had put makeup on to surprise us. We crawled up on Mom's lap scared because she looked so different. It was both funny and scary to see Grandma in makeup as she looked like a clown to us. Nobody we knew at that time wore makeup. We all laughed and she removed it after she saw she had scared us.

Lesson: There's some value in humor and surprise. Look for the light side of scary situations.

20. Learning how to use a rotary phone at my neighbors. I loved going to the neighbors to help clean. I always got to answer the phone when it rang. It took me awhile to understand that each person on the shared party line had a different ring. Sometimes peopled didn't make the two long rings and two short rings just right, and I would end up answering when it was for someone else. It was fun to practice. We didn't have a phone at our house, so it was like a toy.

Lesson: It wasn't long before I learned it's NOT a toy to be played with. It was for farm emergencies or other very important stuff, not for fun. Well I thought it was fun!! When things are new and difficult at first, once learned, they can be appreciated and enjoyed.

FOUR:

The Teen Years Brought Many Changes

"You need to make a commitment, and once you make it, then life will give you some answers."
~ Les Brown

Here are a few short stories from my teen years and the many changes those years brought. I was already starting to use my life lessons and understanding more clearly the value of goal setting and Making A Plan (MAP).

I was failing chemistry at 15 and my teacher told me if I stayed after school two times a week and spent an hour with him trying to understand the subject, he would make sure I passed with at least a D+. He knew I needed the class and a "passing" grade to get into nurses training. So I did so twice a week before I went to the hospital to work as a nurse's aide.

My parents had signed the waiver so I could start to work at age 15. Thus began my life with social security withdrawn. It took me less than a month of working as a nurse's aide to realize that was my calling for sure. I wanted to help people and nursing seemed a perfect fit. I loved every minute of it.

Life Lessons

There are people who want to help; just ask
Determination will help you to meet your goals
Do what it takes to do it right

"Your goals are the road maps that guide you and show you what is possible in your life."
~ Les Brown

Not Smart Enough—Who Would Say That?

The day a teacher told me I wasn't smart enough.

When I announced to my Home Economics teacher my desire to be a nurse, she said, "I don't think your grades are good enough for that; you had better look at other options like a program call LPN, Licensed Practical Nursing, that would suit you better." That's all it took for me to go straight to the school counselor and look into this program versus becoming an RN, Registered Nurse. I believed her, that maybe I wasn't smart enough. I've since learned "other people's opinion of me is none of my business!" To this day I use that in my mind often and sometimes verbalized in a softened way.☺ I simply wanted to get to nursing school and fast. I was ready to leave home and start a life as a young adult on my own.

The school I wanted to attend for my LPN diploma was full for the summer class. I was way behind in registering because of a number of school situations and delays on my part, too. My very best friend had been accepted to start in June right after graduation and that's when I wanted to start too. The Universe works wonderfully. The Administrator of the hospital I worked at was my friend's Dad. The hospital was a Catholic hospital. The same group of nuns who ran the nursing school also ran the hospital I was a nurse's aide at. I wanted to attend with my friend and her Dad made it happen. He assisted the nuns in "deciding" another girl could be moved to the September class and I would be moved to June when his daughter was starting! It worked better for the other girl as well. So I was in and so happy. I received all A's and graduated happy!

My life was very fast paced for a while. I graduated from high school on a Friday, turned 18 on Saturday, left for college on Sunday, and started nurses training Monday. The only downside was my younger brothers and sister were only nine, 10, and 14 and I missed them all a lot. I also knew the situation at home was more volatile than ever and not an easy place to live.

Although it was about 100 miles away, I did come home as often as I could to work at the old hospital I used to work at to help pay my college costs. I would find rides with friends when I could. When I couldn't get home, I worked at the hospital affiliated with the school I was attending. It was a really good time in my life. I was working my way toward something I loved and would provide income for me to take care of myself.

- Other highlights of my late teens years were becoming engaged, graduating from nurses training, getting my real first nursing job and paycheck, renting an apartment with three other girls, and being in my best friend's wedding.

- The most important thing I learned in my late teens was I could take care of myself financially, I was smart, and I had a plan for my future, one I was excited about.

Life Lessons

Know your own worth
Stay strong in what you want in life
Freedom is powerful; use it wisely
It's important to know how smart and valuable you are
Live life fully and love all the speed bumps
Appreciate when someone helps you and sees
your value even if you don't
Be gracious and say thank you with love, smiles,
and doing your best; it feels good

_____
_____
_____
_____
_____
_____
_____
_____

"Each and every day in each and every way my life is getting better and better and better."
~ Richard Maraj, Lead Minister Unity of Phoenix, Phoenix Arizona

FIVE:

Lessons From My Heart

and What I Have Learned

That is Important

"Perfection does not exist—you can always do better and you can always grow."
~ Les Brown

Nana Says, "Lessons From My Heart:
What I Have Learned That's Important.
How do you think these may apply in your life?

• I learned the value and the importance of friendships. Friendship can carry you through the good times and the not-so-good times. Friends will be there for you.

_____
_____
_____
_____
_____
_____

• It's fun to play even as an adult. Learn a sport or activity you can enjoy all your life.

• Music is joyful. Learn to play an instrument for fun. You don't have to be great at it.

• Find comfortable ways and times to talk to your parents/grandparents. Talk about lots of things. Have fun together. Laugh, cry, brag—whatever you want to do.

- You will feel uplifted when you do a community service. It feels good to give back. It's very rewarding and may even be healing.

- Self-confidence and self-esteem will build when you get a job that's appropriate for your age. Learn all you can. This is a time to explore your likes and interests.

- Having a best friend makes life more fun. Sometimes it takes work to find and keep a good friend. Friendship needs to be nurtured as do all relationships. Your investment is worth it.

_____
_____
_____
_____
_____
_____

• It's good to share your stories with those close to you. It's also exciting to share your hopes and dreams. You'll be able to come back to them often to relive, and this is a fun part of life. Allow the people you love to know you.

_____
_____
_____
_____
_____
_____

• Not only is exercise good for you, it can also be enjoyed. You can enjoy a run, walk, bike ride—some activities you can do alone or have fun doing with a friend, maybe even a team. Do something that will help to keep you healthy and happy for life.

___

• There's great value in asking questions when your desire is to gain knowledge and learn. It's just as important to then listen with interest to the answers. This way of learning will help you to grow. It's an important part of your education.

___

• It's important do things you'll remember for a lifetime. Talk about them often. The fun of hearing these stories again and again is they never grow old. They keep getting better.

• Even when doing what you need to do to get something you want may seem difficult at the time and you may not feel like doing it, do it anyway. Keep these three tips in mind: stay happy by smiling often; eliminate the "buts" from your vocabulary, and have something to look forward to.

• It's easy to be kind when we like someone, yet to be kind and respectful to those who are more difficult to be kind to is a bigger challenge. Do it anyway.

• There will be those time when you make a mistake. If you make a mistake, sincerely apologize and move on knowing you did the best you could. We all make mistakes. It's how we handle the mistake after it's made that matters.

• Many times people will share their concerns, hurts, annoyances, painful situations, and more. Simply listen. You don't need to "fix" it. Simply ask, "How may I help?" That's called being kind and gracious—two very important words.

Nana Says! Everything I Know I Learned On The Farm

SIX:

My Life in Balance—

The Steps

"One of the most essential things you need to do for yourself is to choose a goal that is important to you."
~ Les Brown

I was using my life lesson skills even as a child. Yet, it took years before I understood what I did then to make what I wanted to have happen, happen! I made a plan, had a goal, and then nothing could stand in my way. I was clear on my goal! I may not have known what it was at the time; I simply knew it worked.

Today, that's what I teach: the five steps to achieving your goals big or small. It's a process and requires a plan, your own plan.

When using the five steps, you'll discover what's working, what's not, and what holds the highest priority for you today. You'll gain clarity in the area of your life in which you would like to see change or improvement. My five steps outlined below will guide you through the Make A Plan (MAP) process which will move you towards that which you desire

These five steps will help you to achieve your goals. I have note lines for you and encourage you to write your plan down so it's easy to review often.

Make sure to always say "this or something better" as sometimes we think too small and there are bigger plans ahead for us!

1. Identify where you are today in each area of your life in which you would like to see change, improvement, clarity, focus, or maybe learn new skills. This assessment will help you discover where you are today and to discover what's working, what's not working, and where you want improvement. Assess the eight key areas of your life listed below. For each category ask yourself how would you rate yourself today. A number 1 rating indicates that you need and/or desire improvement, while a number 10 rating indicates you're satisfied as is. The number you give each category will help you to decide where you want to focus your attention now to make changes... your place to start. Usually it will be whichever area is your lowest number.

Example: Romance is rated at 2, which means you want improvement. This is the area you want to focus on and see improvement. Your five-step program will be focused on this area for now. It's important to understand that the area you want improvement or change in may change from time to time. As your life changes, you may find other areas in which you want to see improvement. Simply use the same five-step program process.

- Spirituality/Life Purpose
- Romance/Intimacy
- Physical Environment
- Recreation/Fun
- Finances/Money
- Vocation/Job
- Relationships/Family
- Health/Fitness

2. What do you want the area of your life you discovered was needing change or improvement to look like? What is your goal? Be very clear.

_____
_____
_____
_____
_____
_____

3. What are the action steps you need to take to make your goal happen? Think boldly. Date each action step so you have a date to work towards for the change you desire.

___

4. Affirm your goal as though it has already happened. Write this affirmation down and say it often. Saying your affirmation aloud is even better. Post it where you can see it, in your car, bathroom mirror, desk—anywhere you spend time.

___

5. See your goal as achieved. Visualize it with words and pictures. Get excited about the change you want. Find some magazines and cut out words and pictures that represent how you want the goal you identified to look. Be creative. Have fun with it! It's your own personal "vision board" to look at often and imagine life as you desire it.

_____
_____
_____
_____
_____
_____

> *"You may want to change the way you see things rather than trying to change the things you see."*
> ~ Juliet Hubbs and Nora Monaco
> Authors, *Universal Cards Angelically Inspired*

SEVEN:

Testimonials—

My Friends Sharing

Their Thoughts

> *"It's easy to make a buck,*
> *it's tough to make a difference."*
> ~ Tom Brokaw

My life lessons along the way may not have been understood at the time, yet they did impact me. I knew early in my life I wanted to make a difference, a positive difference in people's lives. I found many times as I was confronted with a tough life situation and/or decision, I would ask myself what's the best, the kindest, the healthiest, the smartest way to deal with this situation. It was at those times I knew my life lessons played a significant role. I was prepared and knew what was best. I wanted to make a difference.

I was very excited and humbled when a number of my friends wrote me "love" notes recently for my birthday. The words below that they wrote are not meant to impress you; they're meant to show how each day we have the ability to impact people in a positive way, a way many may remember for years. We may not even know we were impactful at the time.

Here are a few of the love I notes received from friends, and I would like to share them with you.

I remember when I first met you Linda. I knew there was just something about you that made you different from all of the rest. Little did I know not only did you possess great business skills but also the ability to become a dear and treasured friend. I remember our time in Orlando together. We were both navigating thru unchartered waters. In my moments of wondering if I could be as successful as my title, VP of Sales, Linda you just dug in, organized your presentations, made it your business to call and get to know your audience; you became a favorite of my staff and won the admiration of all of those who had the pleasure of being trained by you. Personally, because we had become such good friends I knew your private life was an everyday struggle. I've learned many things from you...most of all how to be a good friend to others, how to count my blessings, how to have fun!!!!! And how to NEVER give up. A treasure you are and always will be and I am looking forward to the day when I can buy your book from the Best Seller List.

Love you, T.

In my many years of knowing Linda, one thing I notice about Linda is that she can and does focus on the lesson learned from situations rather than taking a sour grapes attitude or dwelling on the negative. This allows movement and growth rather than stagnation which I find refreshing and uplifting.

Love, M.

Linda continues to inspire me. From the first time we met I knew she was someone I wanted to have as my friend and I feel very lucky that she is. When she shared her life story with me, the one thing that has stood out as an inspiration to me is her ability to create her own employment and career. There has never been a "No, I can't do that" in her vocabulary. Yes, you can do more than one thing at once and still have balance! Her approach to career and life work has made her very successful and I have learned so much from her and continue to do so every day. She is the true essence of a self-made woman and it is very encouraging. You never see Linda discouraged; she just shifts gears and takes things in stride. If she is ever stressed, it doesn't show. She knows all will work out for the best good. It inspires me to continue in that mindset in my own life. My life is better because you are my friend and someone that I know I can get the straight scoop from in a loving way.

S.

You have done so many things that inspire me. Where do I start?? I think your work ethic and "can do" attitude. I just remember the obstacles put in your way when we were in corporate relocation working together. Oh my, you somehow did not play into the games and continued on your path, your plan. It didn't necessarily always end the way you wanted, but I think made us all stronger. If you could work with the difficult personalities you had to, it seemed you imagined it was just preparing you for the next step.

R.

I can say that what I notice about you Mom is an overall positive outlook and expectation that things will just work out to your liking. You're able to make things happen because you believe that they will happen. The one time that sticks out for me is when Dad moved out. I know that you had a brief moment when you were broken. I had never seen you look so stunned or sad. I also remember how quickly you were able to regain your footing, accept what was happening, and make the decision to move forward. I was very proud of you and it set a good example of how it is okay to fall down as long as you GET BACK UP!

I love you :) xoxo Jennifer

We hope you had a great year and many more to come. My favorite thing we did was when you took us to Del Mar beach. We stayed four hours and I was sunburned in the end, but it was still the best beach day I have ever had. Three things that would describe you are: Smart, Athletic, Fun. Have a great birthday.

Love, Jacob

I would just like to tell you my favorite times in San Diego. I always like seeing the beach and the waves. Seeing you and San Diego is always fun too. I like seeing the bay while talking with you on the porch (and seeing the fireworks sometimes). I like walking on the beach (but walking hurts). Happy B-day!

Love, Sam

I first met Linda when I was working as a realtor in Scottsdale, Arizona. She had come to open a Coldwell Banker relocation office, coordinating incoming moves of corporate transferees. She was working on an innovative project. Linda always seems to have some creative and original project on the drawing board or actually underway. She had realized that transferees coming to a very large metropolitan area, such as Greater Phoenix, should get an overview before focusing too quickly on local neighborhoods. She wanted people to have the whole picture, then learn about the important community resources and unique differences that make urban areas so interesting. I soon found myself using my editorial skills, among other things, helping her to produce a regional resource book. I had grown up in Phoenix and had some sense of the wonderfully different communities and lifestyles that people might learn about in an overview. And, I had been a university editor. The tools Linda developed in this effort meant that individuals and families were less likely to chose an area and a home only later to learn that another nearby community would have been a better choice. I think Linda has an innate sense that the big picture is where you begin, and that an informed process of free and educated choices is most likely to land you where you can flourish.

This praise for Linda as a person who believes in broad overviews has a rather comical biographical aspect—one that I only learned about years into our professional friendship. Linda grew up in South Dakota where she worked on the family farm. This grounded her and gave her many rich experiences, but it was just not what Linda needed to become fully herself. I had known about her rural background (I had spent a few years in Coolidge, Arizona, a cotton-producing town), so I enjoyed hearing stories. We talked about how smart pigs are, and the like. Then in a conversation we got to a major and traumatic event she had never mentioned. She had a daily chore in the chicken coop which was noisy, dark, and unpleasant. One day, along came the wind to slam the coop door shut, and Linda was horrified, trapped inside. She scrambled desperately to get out, finally just breaking down the door. Linda seemed to be in a sweat remembering this story, but was also able to laugh at the end. This was her moment of revelation, she said now she knew she had to leave. She made a plan, eventually moved away, and created a completely different life.

We laughed hard during the telling; nevertheless I also realized that the woman whom I had first met in very sharp, corporate business attire, well-spoken, sophisticated and funny, was a runaway of sorts. She had taken the very frightening experience of being trapped in the dark with upset chickens as her cue to find a bigger, better world outside. She was reborn then, I think.

I learned over time about other unsatisfactory, even dire situations that Linda had confronted, sometimes not just for herself, but for others. As our friendship and our working relationship grew, I learned more about how Linda always liberates herself when the time comes. She loves a challenge and is a natural teacher with a brave and humorous heart. No wonder she enjoys helping others to liberate themselves into happier, more-fulfilling lives.

J.

Words I think of when I think of you are: always available for everyone else, caregiver, extremely capable, very protective of friends, fun loving, motivated, determined, intelligent, beautiful inside and out. There were so many times when you pulled me out of my supposed problems. One I think of was when I was having marital problems and eventually divorced. You were always there to make me feel better about myself. Giving me outlets to get my mind off of things. Letting me move into your home until I found an apartment. Something that a lot of people would not do. You took time to get me out to enjoy things all the while not feeling so good about your own situation. You will never know how much you helped me through that tough time and others. You were always positive. You never asked for favors for yourself. You have accomplished so much in your life and I am very proud of you for that

Love, MK

I have new friends here, but as you know it takes years and years to develop the kind of tried and true friendship you and I have and I've been lucky enough to share with a very few other women. I don't know if we are unusual in that we don't let people go who matter, but I'm very grateful you've hung on to me and I've hung on to you! Our lives are much the same. We are restless with the need to find happy, and happy only comes with risk. When I die, I will not be one of those people who says, "What if?" In fact, even though to some people life moves very fast and suddenly they're "old", I feel as though I've lived two or three lives already. I have no regrets and no feeling of wonder about the things I might have done and didn't. I know you are the same way. I love you my friend, and will always be grateful for your kind words and loving support.

LB

I do remember our first day, starting work at St. Luke's at the time. We were in the bathroom adjusting our caps. I was not really in a good place and not real excited about starting work. I probably was complaining! I remember you saying your husband had left for Vietnam and I thought Wow, if she can do this I certainly should be able to do so. Again you were the cheerleader, just as you continue to be for so many today. Good memory.

Take care! J.

Today John came home with a dozen eggs he bought from a girl at the office who was selling them for dollar a dozen. He said she said they would need to be washed. I quickly asked, "Are you kidding me? I grew up washing 'shit' off of eggs for a penny an egg (or was it a penny a dozen?)." Remember those days at the sink on the farm with no running water? I hated that job!!!!!!

D.

Growing up I always knew I had a second mom to count on. You "took me in", as one of your own and I am very grateful. You provided me with love, words of wisdom, and strength. Growing up I always was in awe of your confidence, your drive, and knowledge of believing that you could follow your dreams without letting fear stand in the way. I have so many memories of your small gestures that for you were probably nothing but to me, meant the world. Like leaving Jennifer and me $10 to get a "treat", or making us popcorn, letting us talk outside on the balcony for hours on end, and providing us with advice, NOT judging us for our (very immature) actions, yet being stern when you needed to be. Still to this day, on Saturday mornings, I wake up, put music on, light a candle, and go to the farmers market for fresh flowers, which always makes me think of you. I love you and am so thankful for you.

N.

Linda and I have been friends for almost 37 years. You have always been my "go to" person when I needed advice or just needed a friend. You have been there for all the joys and sorrows of my life. I am so fortunate to have such a wonderful friend. As you say, we can laugh at nothing and everything! I love you.

K.

Whether you are talking about chips and salsa, tequila and lime, wine and cheese, there are some things that just "go better with…" I am here to say everything goes better with LINDA! From my earliest association reporting to you as my boss to our now Torrey Pines hikes, I have come to cherish our open frank conversations. No topic is too sacred. You "got me" then and still get me today.

B.

Through the years of knowing you we have worked together, played together, and shared sorrow together. You have the unique ability to connect people together who go on to form their own friendships and I know that has given you great pleasure. You are a person of great strength with an even bigger heart for those you care about. You always make being with you fun!

P.

*"Act as if you have already achieved your goals.
Believe that you receive.
Acting with confidence and faith in yourself and your potential sends a powerful message to the universe.
Accept your success right now.
Don't wait until you have actually achieved results.
Act as if...radiating confidence in your ability to achieve them [your dreams] will catapult you forward in your journey."*

~ Edwene Gaines, Author,
The Four Spiritual Laws of Prosperity

About the Author

Linda grew up on a farm in rural South Dakota. Her first career was as a nurse. She learned after a number of years that she would rather be helping people stay healthy by teaching them basic healthy lifestyle techniques.

This started her journey towards a diverse career path from nursing, to real estate sales, to corporate relocation management, to writing *MAP (make a plan) Workbook and Guide* for coaching, to owning and running fitness and weight-loss centers for women.

Linda became a certified Personal Fitness Trainer in 1994 and Life Coach in 2005. She worked with over 2,000 women in her fitness centers to guide them toward meeting their personal fitness and weight loss goals. She currently incorporates coaching into her in balance workshops, individual coaching practice, and volunteer work for women in transition.

Linda's style is one of openness and non-judgment. She's a reality coach who encourages, challenges, and remains grounded. She's passionate in her belief that every human being owes it to themselves to live the best and most fulfilling life possible, and that each of us holds the answers within. Her individual coaching and her workshops are about self-discovery and helping individuals formulate a plan with strategies to get them from where they are to where they want to go with a plan. Their own plan.

Her services include:
Individual Coaching
Workshops
Group Coaching
Speaker at Women's Groups
Onsite Coaching at Women in Transition Centers

To contact her:
lmnickey@aol.com
www.lindanickey.com
925-586-5236

www.ingramcontent.com/pod-product-compliance
Lightning Source LLC
LaVergne TN
LVHW051501070426
835507LV00022B/2865